❖ THE MAUSOLEUM AT
HALICARNASSUS

❖ THE PHAROS LIGHTHOUSE
OF ALEXANDRIA

❖ THE GREAT
PYRAMID OF GIZA

❖ THE SEVEN WONDERS OF THE ANCIENT WORLD

THE TROJAN HORSE

ALBERT LORENZ
WITH **JOY SCHLEH**

Abrams Books for Young Readers
New York

CAST OF CHARACTERS

THE GODS

They want to appear as impartial observers of this human conflict, but each god secretly favors one side or the other, and will intervene to influence the outcome to his or her own satisfaction.

THE GREEKS

On one side are the Greeks from the cities of Athens and Sparta. They wage war against Troy to rescue both Helen and their honor . . .

ZEUS

The King of Everything, the Big Boss, the most powerful god anywhere, anytime. Don't mess with this guy!

HERA

The wife of Zeus, a very beautiful woman, er, goddess.

ARES

God of War: not exactly a happy-go-lucky god, but he does play a central part in our story.

AGAMEMNON

King of the Greeks, the most powerful king on earth. Of course, not as powerful as Zeus.

ACHILLES

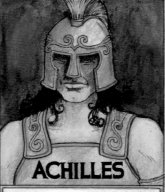

Son of Peleus, a human, and the goddess Thetis, he was immortal unless injured in his heel.

MENELAUS

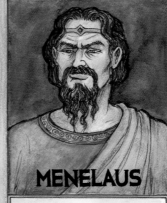

Helen's husband, King of Sparta and brother of Agamemnon.

THE CHORUS

An odd little group that, while not a part of our story, narrates and tells us what is going on.

AJAX

A fierce warrior, a great hero, and a very big guy! (6' 8" tall and 300 lbs.)

HELEN

Daughter of Zeus and Leda, a human, she's the most beautiful woman in the world and Menelaus's wife.

ODYSSEUS

A great Greek warrior, a brilliant strategist, and a very clever fellow.

Throughout the tale, across both pages,

APOLLO

God of the Sun, a bright but dangerous fellow.

APHRODITE

Goddess of Love: if anyone is responsible for this story it's she.

ATHENA

Goddess of Wisdom: when you understand her part in this story you may question that wisdom.

POSEIDON

God of the Sea: he's always moving and he's always all wet.

KRONOS

God of Time: he waits for no one, just ticks along.

THETIS

A minor Goddess, mother of Achilles, the Greek hero.

ERIS

Goddess of Strife: a real troublemaker, she is a very important part of our story.

— THE — TROJANS

. . . On the other side are the citizens and the army of Troy—defending both Helen and their city from the fury of the Greeks . . .

read left to right, then top to bottom.

PRIAM

King of Troy and father of Hector and Paris.

HECTOR

The oldest son of King Priam and the greatest hero of Troy.

MEMNON

King of the Ethiopians and a powerful ally of Troy.

PENTHESILEA

A Trojan ally and Queen of the Amazons—a tribe of fearless women soldiers.

PARIS

Brother of Hector, son of Priam, and kidnapper of Helen—the crime that started it all.

And now our story begins . . .

CAST OF CHARACTERS

"OUR STORY BEGINS ATOP MOUNT OLYMPUS WHERE A WEDDING IS IN FULL SWING. ERIS, THE GODDESS OF STRIFE, HAS NOT BEEN INVITED. RESENTFUL, SHE TOSSES A GOLDEN APPLE INTO THE WEDDING PARTY. THREE GODDESSES—HERA, APHRODITE, AND ATHENA—IMMEDIATELY BEGIN TO QUARREL OVER WHO WILL KEEP THE GOLDEN FRUIT, FOR IT HAS BEEN INSCRIBED: 'FOR THE FAIREST.' NOT WISHING TO MAKE THE CHOICE HIMSELF (AND ANGER TWO OUT OF THREE GODDESSES!), ZEUS ASKS A MERE MORTAL TO MAKE THE CHOICE. HIS NAME IS PARIS."

WELL, OF COURSE IT WAS MEANT FOR ME! I AM UNDENIABLY THE FAIREST.

APHRODITE

WHAT'S WRITTEN ON THE GOLDEN APPLE IS GOING TO CAUSE A STORM.

POSEIDON

MY DEAR, YOU ARE MISTAKEN. THE APPLE IS MINE.

HERA

YOU POOR DEARS. I'M NOT ONLY BRILLIANT, BUT ALSO THE MOST BEAUTIFUL. THE APPLE IS MINE.

ATHENA

"POOR PARIS! THE GODDESSES HAVE TAKEN HUMAN FORM AND ARE PRESSURING HIM!"

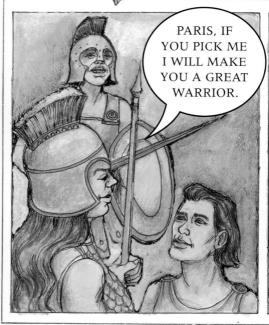

PARIS, IF YOU PICK ME I WILL MAKE YOU A GREAT WARRIOR.

PARIS, IF YOU PICK ME I WILL MAKE YOU A POWERFUL AND WEALTHY MAN.

PARIS, IF YOU PICK ME YOU SHALL HAVE HELEN, THE MOST BEAUTIFUL WOMAN IN THE WORLD!

DON'T WORRY, ZEUS. MY SON, ACHILLES, WILL MAKE SHORT WORK OF THOSE TROJANS.

I COULD START A STORM . . . IF YOU WANTED?

"THOSE ARE HIS COMMANDERS. GUESS IT'S OFFICIAL."

"LOOK! THERE'S ACHILLES! HIS MOTHER BATHED HIM IN THE RIVER STYX WHEN HE WAS AN INFANT, MAKING HIM IMMORTAL. ONLY HIS HEEL WENT UNTOUCHED BY THOSE POWERFUL WATERS."

"WELL, THERE THEY GO. THE WHOLE GREEK ARMY IS SAILING TO TROY TO RESCUE HELEN."

THIS SHIP IS CALLED A TRIREME, AND IT HAS THREE TIERS OF ROWERS (USUALLY SLAVES) WORKING UNDER VERY HARSH CONDITIONS—ONLY THOSE ON THE TOP LEVEL COULD EVEN SEE THE WATER.

TRIREMES CARRIED SOLDIERS ARMED WITH SPEARS, SWORDS, AND SHIELDS SO THAT THEY COULD FIGHT ON LAND AS WELL AS AT SEA.

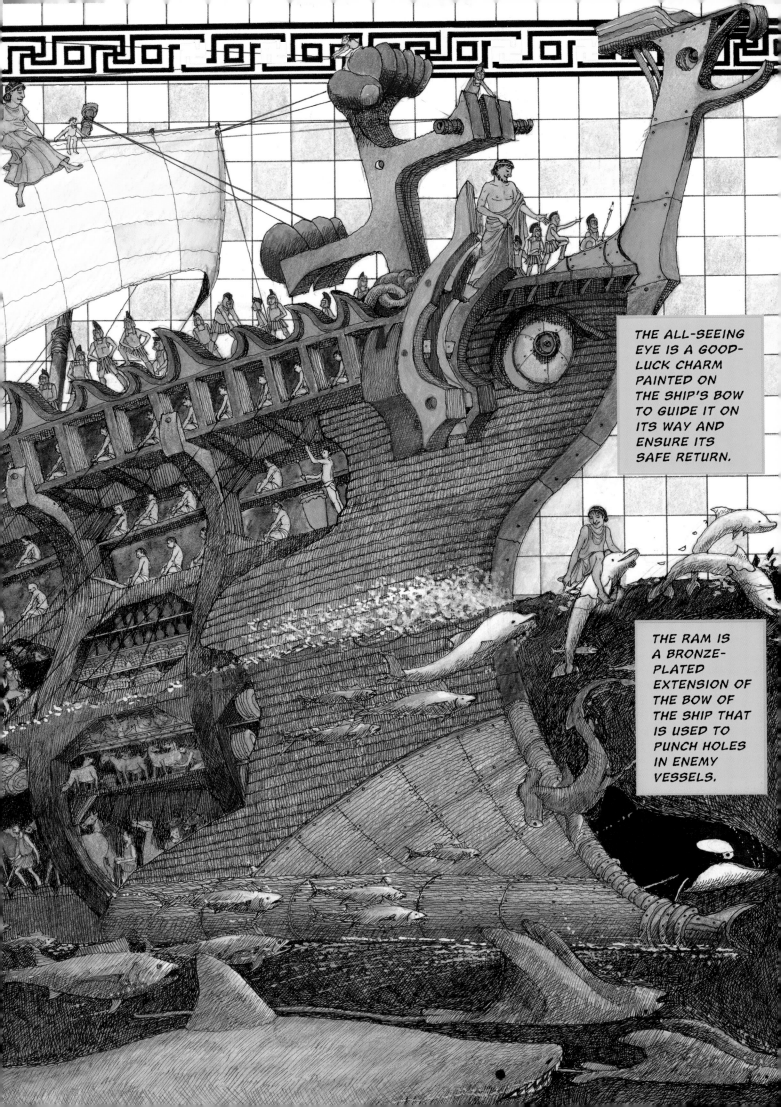

THE ALL-SEEING EYE IS A GOOD-LUCK CHARM PAINTED ON THE SHIP'S BOW TO GUIDE IT ON ITS WAY AND ENSURE ITS SAFE RETURN.

THE RAM IS A BRONZE-PLATED EXTENSION OF THE BOW OF THE SHIP THAT IS USED TO PUNCH HOLES IN ENEMY VESSELS.

THE TOWER
OF ILIOS

WEAVING WOOL CLOTH
WAS ONE OF TROY'S VERY
PROFITABLE INDUSTRIES.

SIGNS OF THE EVER-PRESENT READINESS
FOR WAR AND DEFENSE OF THE CITY ARE
OBVIOUS FROM THE SOLDIERS AND THE
STORAGE FACILITIES IN THE LOWER LEVELS.

THIS SIEGE IS TAKING YEARS!

WE NEED SOME ACTION!

LET'S SEND HECTOR OUT TO CHALLENGE ACHILLES TO COMBAT.

ZEUS

ARES

ERIS

"THE GATES ARE OPEN, BUT ONLY HECTOR STEPS OUTSIDE. WHAT'S UP? HECTOR, THE SON OF TROY'S KING PRIAM, IS CHALLENGING ACHILLES TO SINGLE COMBAT. IF HE CAN BEAT ACHILLES, THE WAR MIGHT BE OVER. DOESN'T HE KNOW ACHILLES IS INVINCIBLE?"

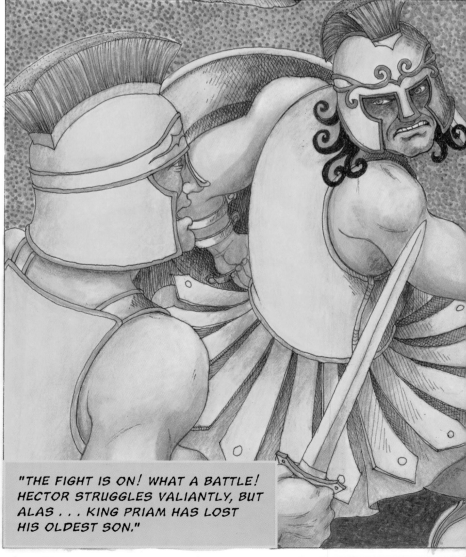

"THE FIGHT IS ON! WHAT A BATTLE! HECTOR STRUGGLES VALIANTLY, BUT ALAS . . . KING PRIAM HAS LOST HIS OLDEST SON."

I COULD START A STORM . . . IF YOU WANTED?
POSEIDON
I WOULDN'T DO THAT IF I WERE YOU. MY SON IS UNBEATABLE.
THETIS
OH, BE QUIET ABOUT A STORM!
ATHENA

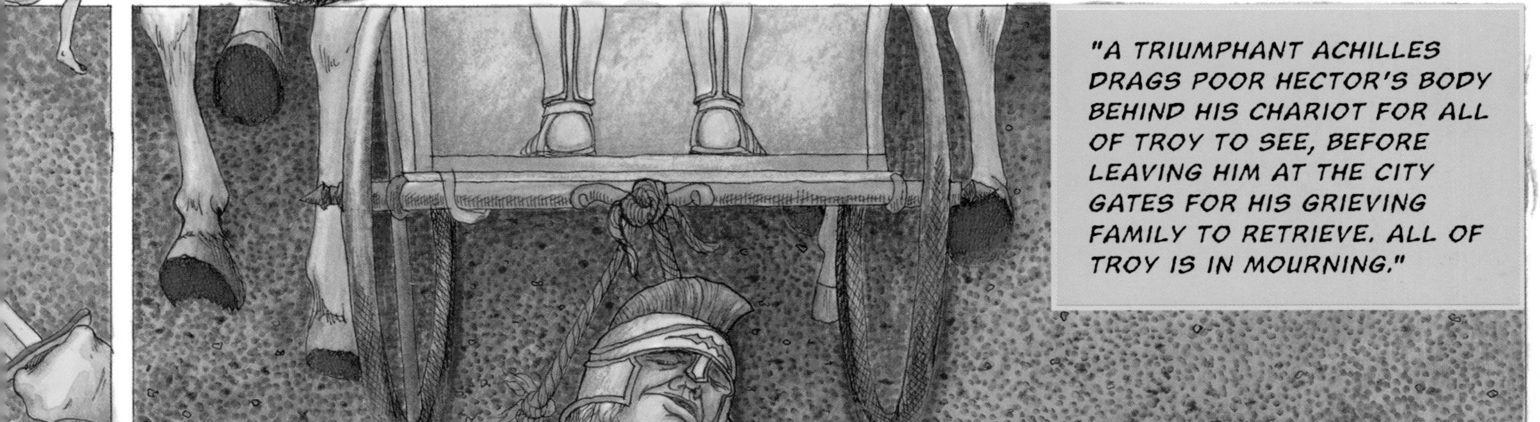
"A TRIUMPHANT ACHILLES DRAGS POOR HECTOR'S BODY BEHIND HIS CHARIOT FOR ALL OF TROY TO SEE, BEFORE LEAVING HIM AT THE CITY GATES FOR HIS GRIEVING FAMILY TO RETRIEVE. ALL OF TROY IS IN MOURNING."

LOOK AT THE TROJANS—THEY CONTINUE TO BATTLE! THEY ARE NOT GIVING AN INCH!
THIS SIEGE HAS GONE ON FOR ALMOST TEN YEARS!
WELL . . . IF YOU WOULD GIVE THEM A LITTLE HELP . . .
"DO YOU SEE WHO IS COMING TO HELP TROY IN HER HOUR OF NEED? IT'S THE AMAZON QUEEN, PENTHESILEA, AND HER ARMY."
"BUT PENTHESILEA IS NO MATCH FOR ACHILLES."
"PARIS HAS TAKEN HIS BOW. HE IS AIMING IT AT ACHILLES! WHO IS THAT HELPING HIM AIM THE BOW? IT'S APOLLO! HE HAS TAKEN THE FORM OF AN OWL!"
"PARIS'S ARROW FINDS ITS TARGET."

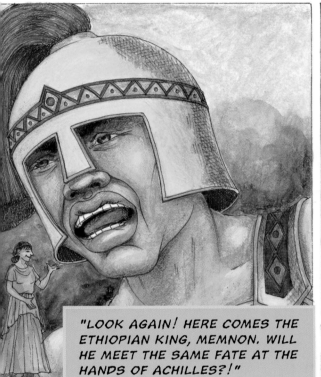

"LOOK AGAIN! HERE COMES THE ETHIOPIAN KING, MEMNON. WILL HE MEET THE SAME FATE AT THE HANDS OF ACHILLES?!"

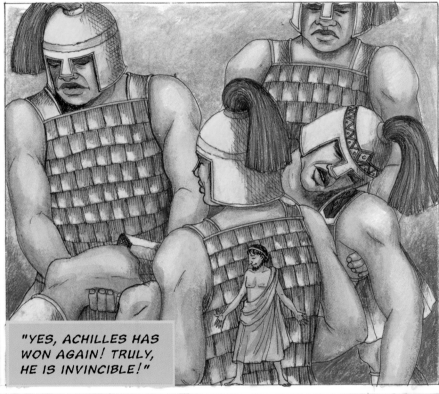

"YES, ACHILLES HAS WON AGAIN! TRULY, HE IS INVINCIBLE!"

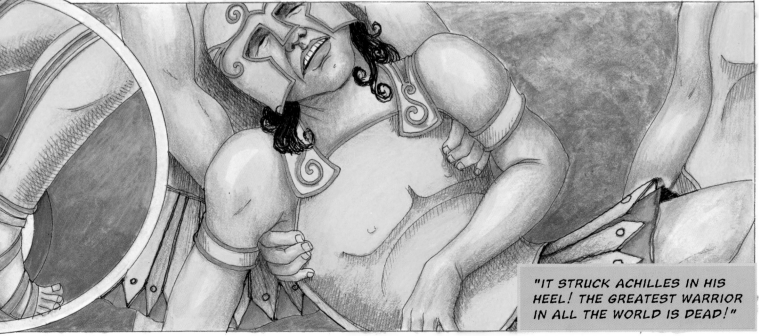

"IT STRUCK ACHILLES IN HIS HEEL! THE GREATEST WARRIOR IN ALL THE WORLD IS DEAD!"

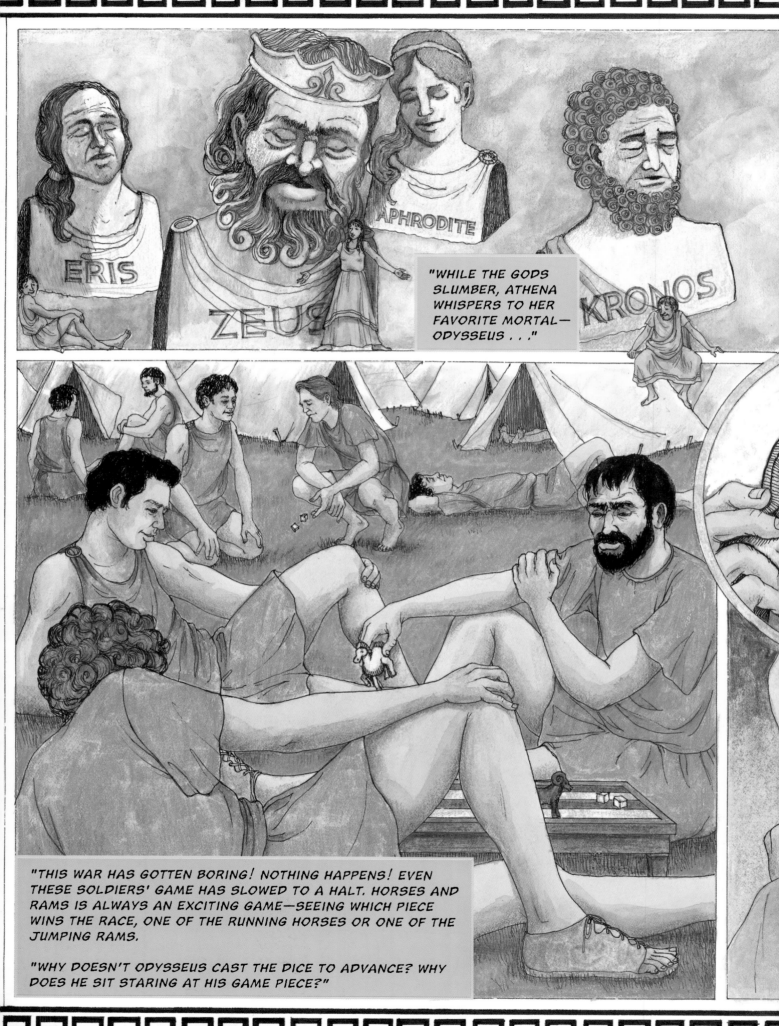

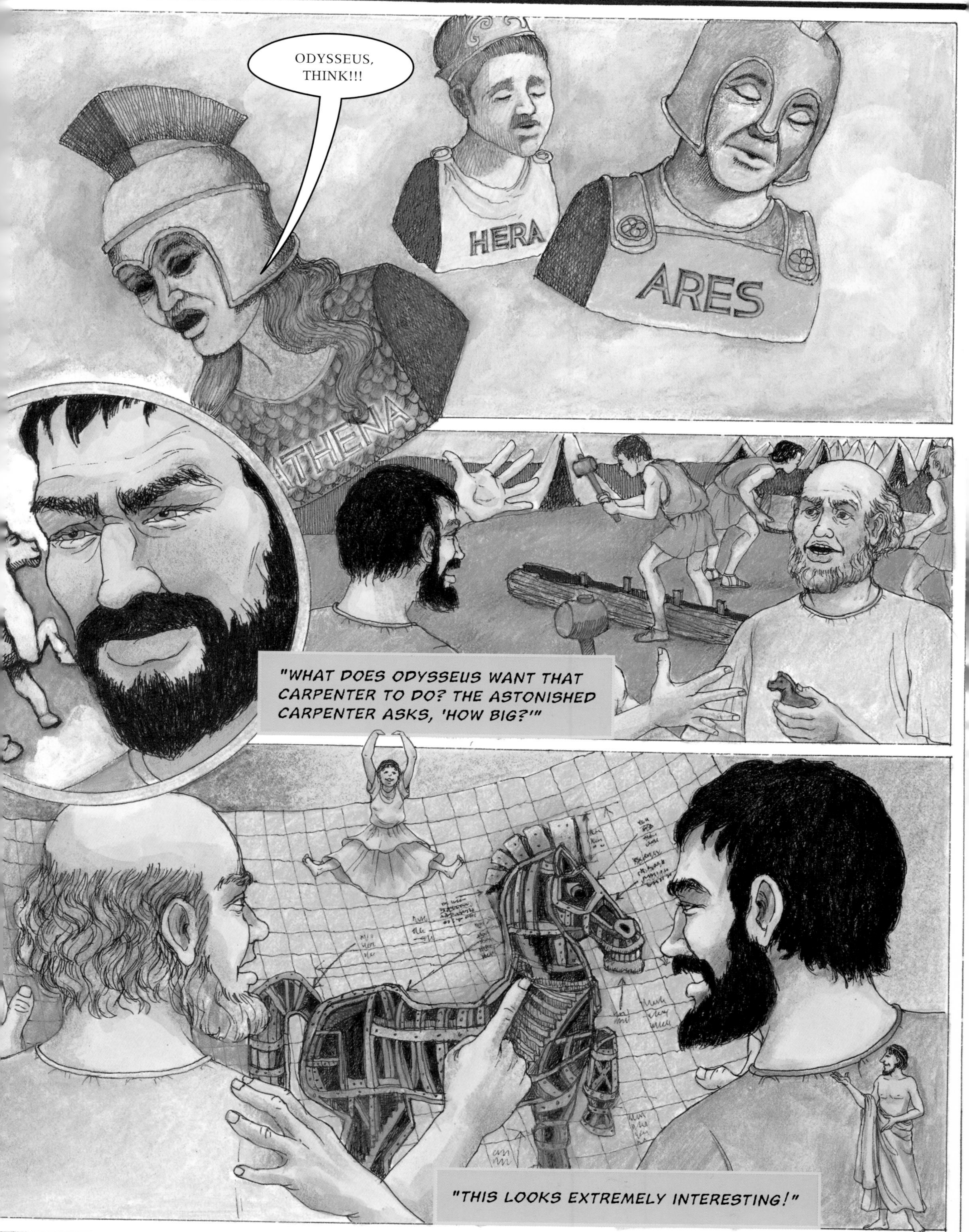
ODYSSEUS, THINK!!!
HERA
ARES
ATHENA
"WHAT DOES ODYSSEUS WANT THAT CARPENTER TO DO? THE ASTONISHED CARPENTER ASKS, 'HOW BIG?'"
"THIS LOOKS EXTREMELY INTERESTING!"

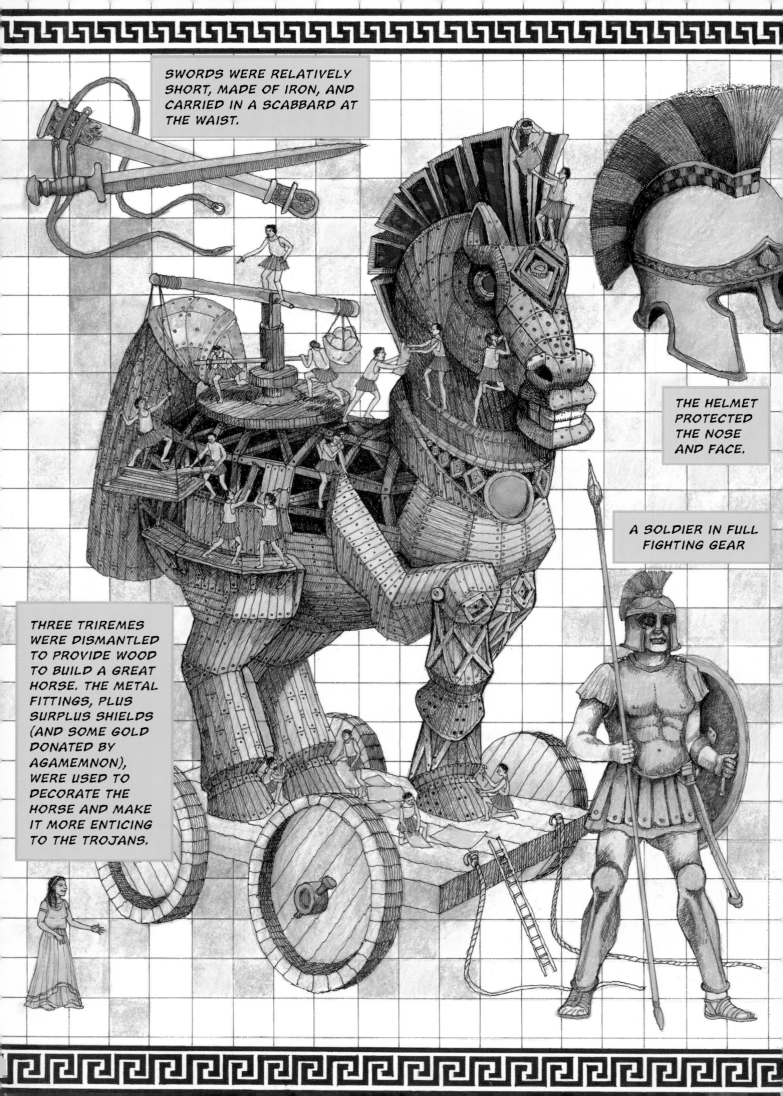

SWORDS WERE RELATIVELY SHORT, MADE OF IRON, AND CARRIED IN A SCABBARD AT THE WAIST.

THE HELMET PROTECTED THE NOSE AND FACE.

A SOLDIER IN FULL FIGHTING GEAR

THREE TRIREMES WERE DISMANTLED TO PROVIDE WOOD TO BUILD A GREAT HORSE. THE METAL FITTINGS, PLUS SURPLUS SHIELDS (AND SOME GOLD DONATED BY AGAMEMNON), WERE USED TO DECORATE THE HORSE AND MAKE IT MORE ENTICING TO THE TROJANS.

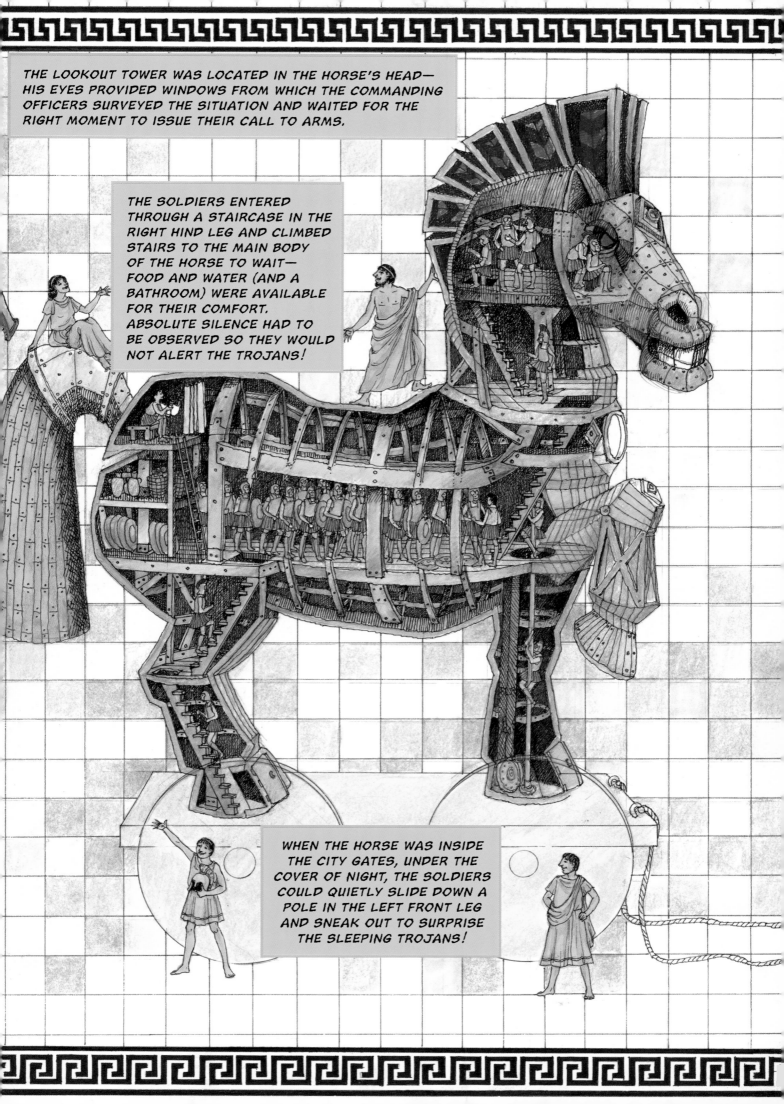

THE LOOKOUT TOWER WAS LOCATED IN THE HORSE'S HEAD—HIS EYES PROVIDED WINDOWS FROM WHICH THE COMMANDING OFFICERS SURVEYED THE SITUATION AND WAITED FOR THE RIGHT MOMENT TO ISSUE THEIR CALL TO ARMS.

THE SOLDIERS ENTERED THROUGH A STAIRCASE IN THE RIGHT HIND LEG AND CLIMBED STAIRS TO THE MAIN BODY OF THE HORSE TO WAIT—FOOD AND WATER (AND A BATHROOM) WERE AVAILABLE FOR THEIR COMFORT. ABSOLUTE SILENCE HAD TO BE OBSERVED SO THEY WOULD NOT ALERT THE TROJANS!

WHEN THE HORSE WAS INSIDE THE CITY GATES, UNDER THE COVER OF NIGHT, THE SOLDIERS COULD QUIETLY SLIDE DOWN A POLE IN THE LEFT FRONT LEG AND SNEAK OUT TO SURPRISE THE SLEEPING TROJANS!

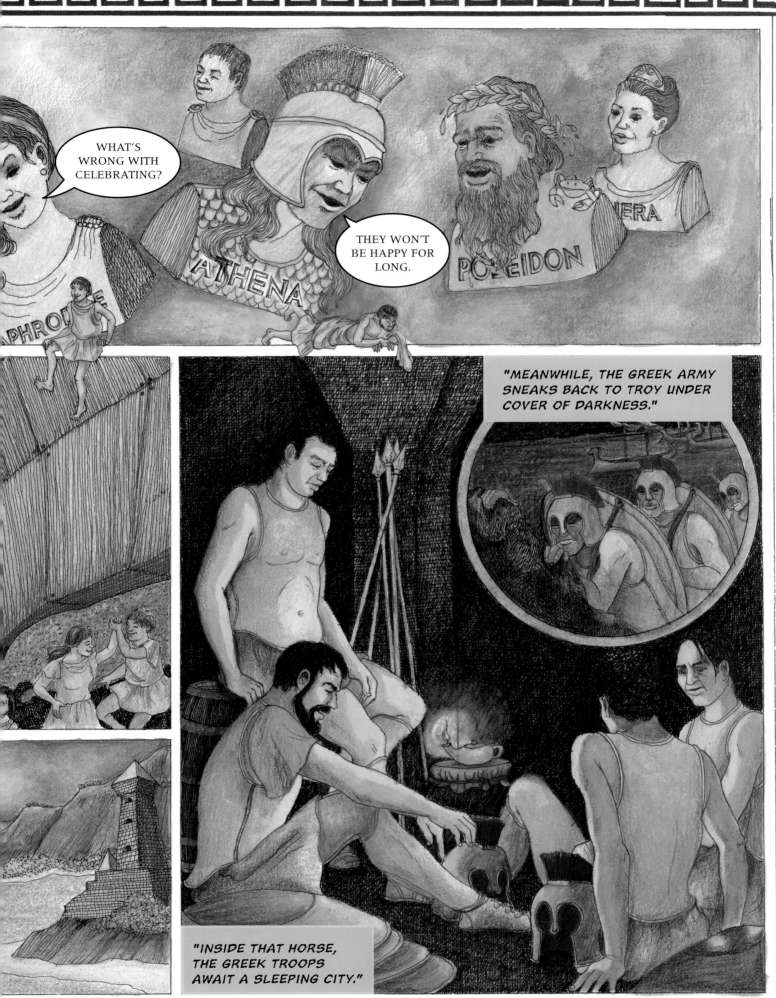

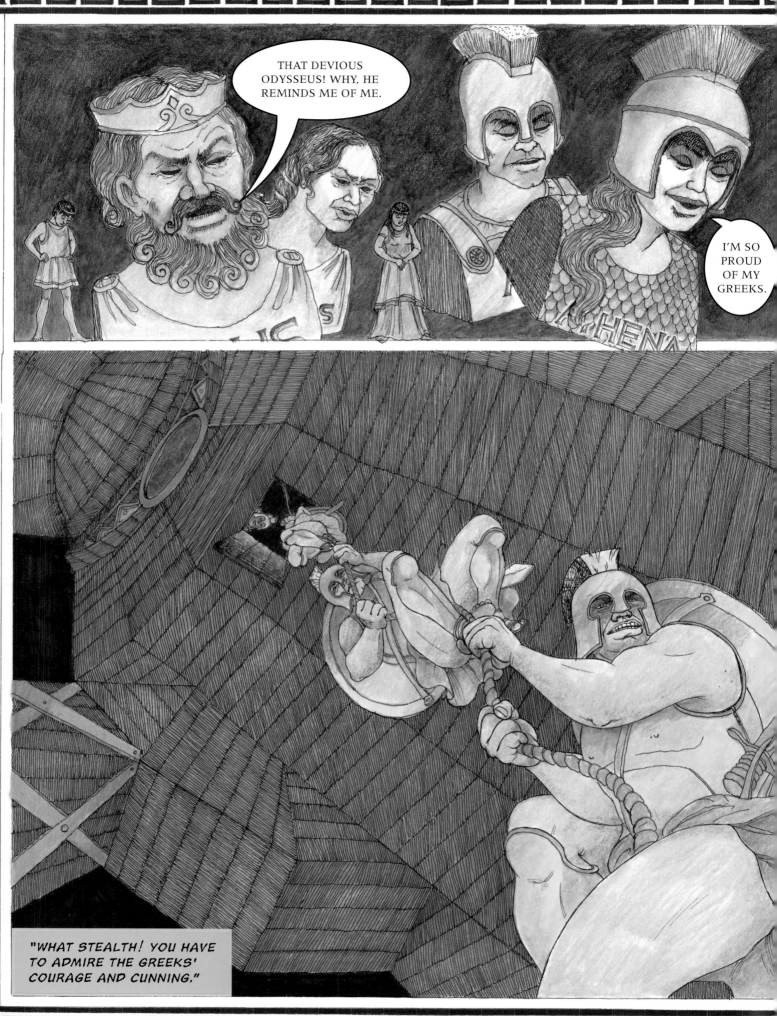

"THAT, MY FRIENDS, IS THE END OF THE TROJAN WAR."

AUTHOR'S NOTE

Most people have heard of or know about the Seven Wonders of the Ancient World. The possibility that the city of Troy and the Seven Wonders of the Ancient World most likely existed at the same time has always intrigued me. The idea that the Pharos Lighthouse of Alexandria and the last city of Troy were both destroyed during the same era, approximately 1000 CE, especially fascinated me as a young architect interested in ancient cultures.

The first city of Troy was built along the shores of the Aegean Sea in approximately 3000 BCE, the same time that the Great Pyramids were constructed. During the next four thousand years, the city of Troy was destroyed and rebuilt at least ten times. Although the existence of Troy is acknowledged historically, there are no drawings, models, or extensive ruins on which to base a visual re-creation. The Troy of which Homer wrote is believed to have existed between 1500 and 1300 BCE, and so I used those dates as my basis.

In order to draw the city, I researched architectural history and searched for buildings and cities built at that time. To come up with a comparable visual likeness, I used Bronze Age architecture, specifically Minoan architecture, as my model. This type of architecture consists of massive stone walls, beautifully carved and requiring no mortar since each stone fits perfectly. This method is called Ashlar masonry. The inside of the walls was plastered and then painted with colorful murals. Ancient Greek vases provided me with the style of dress for the Greeks and Trojans.

Reading Greek myths, especially about the gods, helped me to get a feel for the people and what they had to put up with! I was astounded to learn that via the oral tradition of passing tales from generation to generation the legend of the Trojan Horse was famous long before Homer wrote *The Iliad* and *The Odyssey*. For today's readers these epics immortalized the gods and the city of Troy.

The map of the ancient world that is illustrated on the endpapers of this book shows where the city of Troy was probably located. Each new Troy was built on the wreckage of the previous one. During this time, the Seven Wonders of the Ancient World were also built.

The Great Pyramids were built in 3000 BCE.

The Hanging Gardens of Babylon were built in 900 BCE.

The Statue of Zeus was built in 500 BCE.

The Temple of Artemis was built in 600 BCE.

The Mausoleum at Halicarnassus was built in 400 BCE.

The Colossus at Rhodes was built in 400 BCE.

The Pharos Lighthouse of Alexandria was built in 300 BCE.

Homer's Troy existed during the Classical Period, a time famous for celebrating physical beauty. The sculpture of the period depicts gods that were idealized and perfectly formed. In myths these gods manipulated humans as they would puppets. I visualized them floating above the human world, amusing themselves. I portrayed them as stone busts because that was the way I viewed them when visiting museums or reading books on ancient Greece. Very solid!

I incorporated an ancient Greek theatrical element—the chorus—to join the gods in telling the story. The chorus fills in gaps in the story and gives pertinent background information, helping to move the story along, just as it does in ancient plays.

My research for this book was extensive, and my architectural background helped me immensely. Susan Woodford's book, *The Trojan War in Ancient Art* (Cornell University Press, 1993), and *The Seven Wonders of the Ancient World*, edited by Peter A. Clayton and Martin Price (Routledge, 1988), were also very useful. And last but not least, thank you very much, Homer.

Joy Schleh and I collaborated on this book as we have on others in the past. I create a rough draft and page layouts. We then go through several stages of critiques, sending the drawings back and forth between us. Through this method the drafts and sketches take on new layers and eventually we have the final artwork— work with which we are both satisfied and believe best exemplifies our original intent. It is an exhausting process, but fun!

Designer: Vivian Cheng
Production Manager: Alexis Mentor

Library of Congress Cataloging-in-Publication Data has been applied for.
ISBN 10: 0-8109-5986-0
ISBN 13: 978-0-8109-5986-6

Printed and bound in Singapore
10 9 8 7 6 5 4 3 2 1

HNA ▮▯▯▮▯

THE TEMPLE
OF ARTEMIS
AT EPHESUS

Troy

THE STATUE OF
ZEUS AT OLYMPIA

GREECE   Athens

Sparta

THE COLOSSUS
OF RHODES

ZEUS

MEDITERRANEAN SEA

APHRODITE

THE WORLD of the
GREEKS AND TROJANS